# From My Poetic Heart

*by*
*L. Diane Hindman*

LifeHouse
Publishing
Littleton, CO

Copyright 2010 by L. Diane Hindman

Published by LifeHouse Publishing, LLC
LifeHouse Publishing

LifeHouse Publishing, its logo and any marks are trademarks of LifeHouse Publishing

Cover Design: Joe Kroog
Design and Layout: Jill Kroog and Joe Kroog
Illustrations: Joe Kroog
Typesetting: Jill Kroog
Photography: L. Diane Hindman

All rights reserved. This publication, in part or in whole, may not be reproduced, stored in a retrieval system, or transmitted in any form or by any means - electronic, mechanical, photocopying, recording or otherwise, without the written permission of the publisher.

Library of Congress Control Number available from Library of Congress

Hindman, L. Diane
    From My Poetic Heart: Four volumes of poetry from the heart - Heartstrings, Heartbeats, Heartfelt, and Heart-2-Heart

# Table of Contents

## Heartstrings

| | |
|---|---|
| Heartstrings | 3 |
| Darkness Before Dawn | 4 |
| First Day | 5 |
| Growing Up | 5 |
| Endless Love | 5 |
| Do You Love Me? | 6 |
| Anniversary | 6 |
| Wild Geese | 7 |
| Kelly | 7 |
| Katelynn | 8 |
| My Love | 8 |
| Memories | 9 |
| I Do | 10 |
| All Grown Up | 10 |
| Freedom's Sacrifice | 11 |
| Words of Love | 12 |
| Forgotten | 12 |
| Best Friends | 13 |
| The Gift | 14 |
| Little Golden Head | 15 |
| Cuddle Me? | 15 |
| Father's Lament | 16 |
| A Grandma's Prayer | 16 |
| Feline Friendship | 17 |
| Angel in Disguise | 18 |
| Pictures | 19 |
| Angel Face | 19 |
| Wedded Bliss | 20 |
| Missing You | 20 |
| Partners | 21 |
| Friendship | 22 |
| Second Chance | 22 |
| Aspen Gold | 23 |
| Happy Face | 24 |
| Mother's Love | 24 |
| Second Child | 25 |
| Always My Child | 25 |
| Time for the Heart | 26 |
| Guardian Angel | 26 |
| Soul Mates | 27 |
| The Music of Memory | 27 |

## Heartbeats

| | |
|---|---|
| Heartbeats | 31 |
| Treasures | 31 |
| My Closest Friend | 31 |
| Masquerade | 32 |
| Christmas Joy | 32 |
| Hollyhock Dolls | 33 |
| Rainy Day | 33 |
| Make Me Worthy | 34 |
| Sky Hunter | 35 |
| Love Ties | 36 |
| Unsung Heroes | 36 |
| Think It Over | 37 |
| Among the Angels | 37 |
| Unicorn | 38 |
| Memory's Garden | 38 |
| The Visit | 39 |
| Forgiveness | 39 |
| Armchair Traveler | 40 |
| Grandmother's Ring | 41 |
| I Remember Mimi | 41 |
| Poppa's Stories | 42 |
| By the Windmill | 43 |
| "Getting On" | 44 |
| Too Many Words for Blue | 44 |
| Rabbits' Dance | 45 |
| Farewell | 46 |
| Child of Stone | 46 |
| Silent Servants | 47 |
| Please Stay | 48 |
| Life Goes On | 48 |
| Transition | 49 |
| Nests | 50 |
| I Can Fly | 51 |
| Cherubs | 52 |
| Music | 52 |
| Tribute | 53 |
| The Storm | 54 |
| It's Over | 55 |
| Eternal Vow | 55 |
| The Wall | 56 |
| Comfort Me | 57 |
| With Each Beat | 57 |

# Table of Contents - Continued

## Heartfelt

| | |
|---|---:|
| Heartfelt | 61 |
| Sacrifice | 61 |
| Grandchildren | 62 |
| When I Loved You | 62 |
| The Hug | 63 |
| A Perfect Stranger | 63 |
| The Sounds of Freedom | 64 |
| I Wish For You | 65 |
| By Myself | 66 |
| White Lilacs | 66 |
| When Love Died | 67 |
| Touch My Heart | 67 |
| Ode to Katie's Eyes | 68 |
| Loneliness | 69 |
| Then and Now | 69 |
| It Doesn't Hurt Anymore | 70 |
| Remember I Love You | 70 |
| Apology | 71 |
| Tears in My Heart | 71 |
| Going Home at Last | 72 |
| Heroes | 73 |
| Door to the Future | 74 |
| The Eyes of Your Soul | 74 |
| The Rarest Flower | 75 |
| Shadows | 76 |
| Our Love Will Last | 77 |
| Bonds of Love | 77 |
| You Are My Brother | 78 |
| Old Friends | 78 |
| Did I Fail? | 79 |
| I Chose you | 79 |
| Broken Pieces | 80 |
| Hearts of Steel | 80 |
| Walk in the Snow | 81 |
| Freedom's Flag | 82 |
| Heart Songs | 83 |
| No Goodbyes | 83 |
| Little Brother | 84 |
| WTC Remembered | 84 |
| Love is a River | 85 |

## Heart-2-Heart

| | |
|---|---:|
| Heart to Heart | 89 |
| Kaleidoscope | 89 |
| A Sweetness of Heart | 90 |
| Across the Miles | 91 |
| The One Who Loves You | 92 |
| Way Back When | 92 |
| Cowboy Dreams | 93 |
| Reunion | 94 |
| Lest We Forget | 95 |
| Preservation | 96 |
| Meditation | 97 |
| Easter Prayer | 97 |
| Your Best Friend | 98 |
| What is in Your Heart? | 98 |
| Help Me, Lord | 99 |
| Open My Eyes | 100 |
| Redemption | 100 |
| My Prayer | 101 |
| A Light in the Dark | 102 |
| Regret | 102 |
| If God Made Eve First | 103 |
| Betrayed | 104 |
| Only a Dream | 104 |
| Storms | 105 |
| I Pray for You | 106 |
| The Traveler's Dream | 107 |
| First Teacher's Conference | 108 |
| Carousel | 109 |
| Three Wishes | 110 |
| School Dance | 111 |
| Columbia | 112 |
| All Hallow's Eve | 113 |
| Island in the Sun | 114 |
| Renewed Trust | 115 |
| Come Back to Me | 116 |
| Let Go and Let God | 117 |

# Dedication

This book is dedicated to:

My grandmother, Mimi, who was a poet in her own right and my muse.

My husband, Jim, because he always believed in me and likes my poems.

My children and grandchildren who were the inspiration for many of these poems.

And to all of you readers who have made my dream come true by reading these verses from my poetic heart.

# Heartstrings

*In happy times and sad, in laughter and in tears, there are poignant moments in our lives that tug at our hearts.*

*These flashes of memory stay with us down the years to come back unexpectedly with crystal clarity. They may be sparked by the sound of a baby's laugh, tears in the eyes of a child, an old photograph, the perfume of a flower, a snatch of the melody you danced to. If we could only capture these small vignettes to take them out from time to time to savor again and again.*

*This collection of poems has been my way of holding on to those special times in life that I want to remember always and treasure forever; moments that play like music on my heartstrings.*

L. Diane Hindman

# Heartstrings

*A gentle touch, a smiling face,*
*A lovely child who moves with grace,*
*Memories, gathered down the years,*
*Remembrances of joy and tears.*

*The ache that caused my heart to throb*
*With each painful, wrenching sob,*
*Your little, tinkling, crystal laugh*
*As you skipped down the garden path.*

*The morning sun upon the grass,*
*The whispering breezes drifting past,*
*A baby's sigh when fast asleep,*
*The warmth of purple shadows deep.*

*Flowers blooming in the spring,*
*A lark that sings while on the wing,*
*The bounty of God's endless love,*
*Salvation sent from Heaven above.*

*I hoard these thoughts, these precious things,*
*Like music played upon my heartstrings.*

## Darkness Before Dawn

It's always dark before the dawn.
God gives us strength to carry on.
When nothing seems to be worthwhile,
The sun shines in your children's smile.

And darling, even though it seems
There's only darkness in your dreams,
Those tears within your heart will be
Turned to diamonds, and you'll see
That hope and love and truth prevail,
Even when we seem to fail.

God gives us strength to carry on
And greet with joy the breaking dawn.

## First Day

*She stood there smiling up at me,
And it touched my heart to see
How much my little girl had grown,
This last summer, here at home.*

*She kissed my cheek, then out the door,
And I knew, forevermore,
This was the last time I would see
The baby that she used to be.*

*Granting me a backward glance,
And before I had a chance
To dry the tears that stained my face,
She skipped away with gangly grace.*

*Now, other interests there would be,
And she will have less time for me.
With heavy heart, I watched my jewel,
Leave for her first day of school.*

## Growing Up

*He looked so small standing there,
With shining face and slicked down hair.
Excitement glowed within his eyes,
As if life held some great surprise.*

*He laughed at me with childish glee,
As I knelt on bended knee
To wrap him in a last embrace,
And memorize his upturned face.*

*His baby days were left behind,
To live on only in my mind,
As I watched him skip away
To go to school on his first day.*

## Endless Love

*Like the circle of a ring,
Love itself is an endless thing.
A sphere of continuity,
Tightly binds your heart to me.*

*With no beginning, without end,
I will forever be your friend.
Yours in perpetuity,
Love lasts beyond infinity.*

# Do You Love Me?

*Do you love me after all these years,*
*Even when causing you pain and tears?*
*In spite of all my foolish mistakes?*
*Because, sweetheart, that's what loving takes.*

*Do you love me when I'm silly and weak,*
*Or when I'm glum and refuse to speak?*
*When I'm wrong and don't know what to say,*
*Will you still love me the same old way?*

*Do you love me, darling, with all my faults,*
*And when I'm riddled with niggling doubts?*
*I pray to heaven that you still do,*
*Because, my dearest, I love you too.*

# Anniversary

*Together, we've stood side by side,*
*Since I became your blushing bride*
*And you agreed to be my groom.*
*In our lives we made some room*
*For little ones who've grown and gone.*
*There's just we two to carry on.*

*Year by year and day by day,*
*Our life has gone upon its way.*
*We've shared our laughter and our tears.*
*We've told each other all our fears.*
*Through both the good times, and some bad,*
*We're grateful for the times we've had.*

*We've reached our anniversary date,*
*The day when we combined our fate.*
*Each year we celebrate again,*
*And reminisce just where we've been.*
*And so, we've shared another year,*
*And I'm still beside you, dear.*

# Wild Geese

*High above, their haunting cry*
*Echoes through the pristine sky.*
*My soul yearns upward at their call,*
*Longing on this day in fall*
*To fly with them to foreign parts.*
*I feel the freedom in their hearts.*
*But, as they pass overhead,*
*I turn my face toward home, instead.*

# Kelly

*With laughing eyes and shining face,*
*Pixie grin and elfin grace,*
*Kelly sets my life aglow.*
*Just her presence fills me so*
*With love that I can hardly stand.*
*She holds my heart within her hand.*

*Grandmas often brag and boast,*
*But Kelly really is the most*
*Darling and endearing child,*
*Winsome, sweet and gaily wild.*
*Happy, loving all day through,*
*I find her charming. Wouldn't you?*

# Katelynn

She knows not she's an angel,
Sent from Heaven above.
A precious little bundle,
To cherish and to love.

She'll hold your heart within
Her tiny baby hand.
Your life will have more blessings,
Than the sea has sand.

Always, you'll remember,
The moment of her birth,
When God loaned you an angel,
To fill your world with mirth.

The happiness she'll bring you,
Is a glimpse of heavenly bliss,
With all that's good compressed
Into a single baby kiss.

## My Love

Light of my life, heart of my heart,
My best friend, where do I start
To tell you what you mean to me?
Being with you sets my spirit free.

You were my love when we were young,
When our life together had just begun.
And now, as gray streaks our hair,
By God's grace, you'll always be there.

The passion that flared is now a glow
Of the lasting love we've come to know.
So, when I smile and come to you,
Please answer me, "I love you too".

## Memories

*Memories bring feelings warm
In which I wrap myself.
I place each one lovingly
Upon a mental shelf,
To wait until I need again
To savor its recall,
Cherishing the minutes past,
It matters not how small.*

*They hold the fabric of our lives
Together like a thread,
Rather like a favorite book
From time to time reread.
A memory has value
Like a rare and precious jewel,
If anyone denies this truth,
May he be branded 'fool'.*

*As life rushes by us
At a wild and hectic pace,
We may feel suspended
In an empty space.
No matter what befalls us
Or what others take away,
Our memories are ours to keep,
Forever and a day.*

# I Do

On our dawning wedding day,
Your smile tells more than words
can say.
Reflected in your eyes I see,
A special love for only me.

Our lives are now so entwined,
We speak and think as if one mind.
Inseparable our lives will be,
Partners for eternity.

You are my life, my love, my soul,
The other half that makes me whole.
And so I pledge my all to you,
With these two little words, "I do".

## All Grown Up

You're not a child,
But a woman grown,
With home and husband
And babes of your own.
No more a small girl
With golden hair,
But a lovely young woman,
Gentle and fair.
The days are gone
When I kissed your knee,
Or admired the pictures
You brought to me.
The years have flown
So swiftly by,
"Please bring them back."
I sadly cry.
But when all is said
And done, in the end,
You're more than my daughter,
You're my best friend.

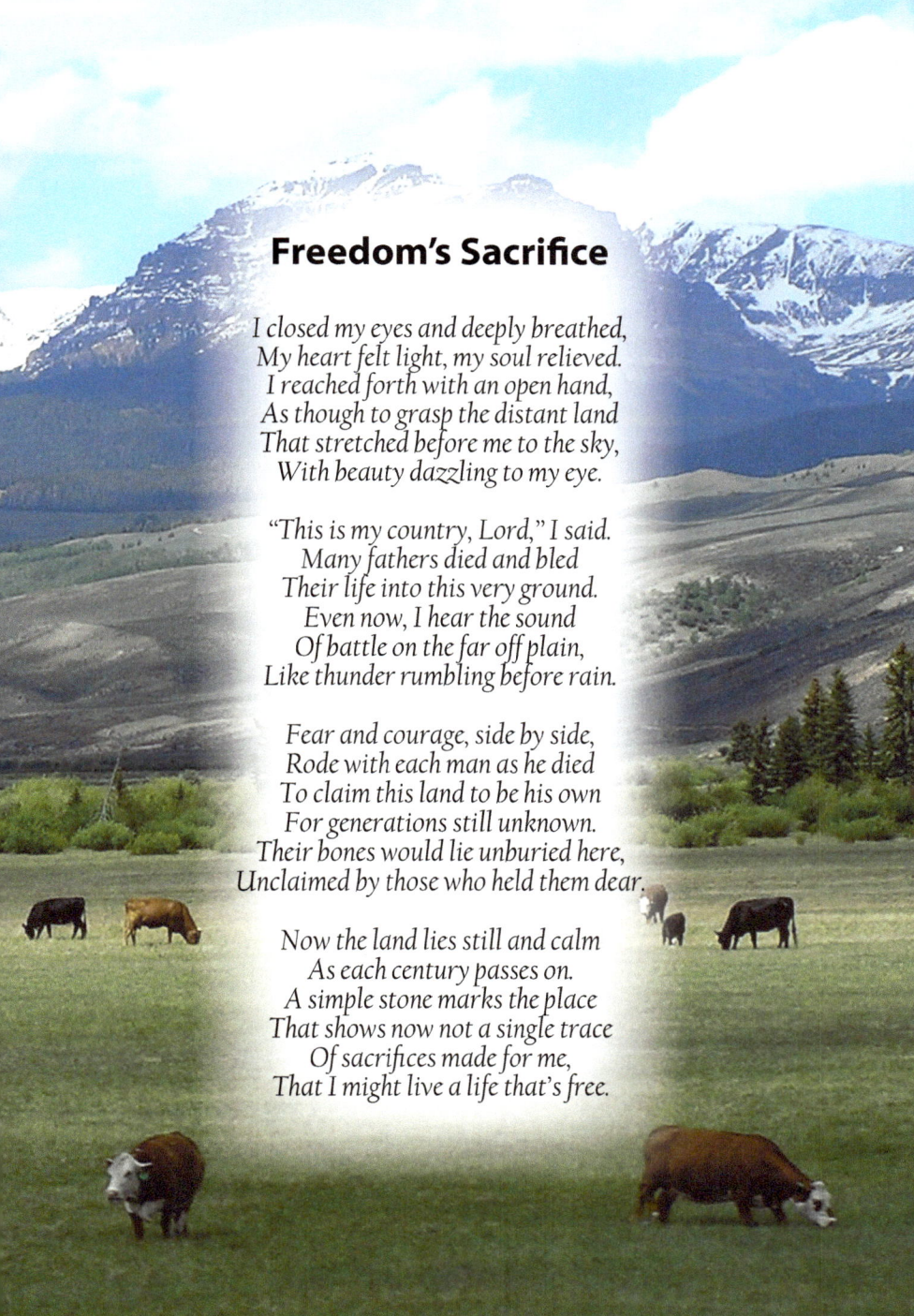

# Freedom's Sacrifice

I closed my eyes and deeply breathed,
My heart felt light, my soul relieved.
I reached forth with an open hand,
As though to grasp the distant land
That stretched before me to the sky,
With beauty dazzling to my eye.

"This is my country, Lord," I said.
Many fathers died and bled
Their life into this very ground.
Even now, I hear the sound
Of battle on the far off plain,
Like thunder rumbling before rain.

Fear and courage, side by side,
Rode with each man as he died
To claim this land to be his own
For generations still unknown.
Their bones would lie unburied here,
Unclaimed by those who held them dear.

Now the land lies still and calm
As each century passes on.
A simple stone marks the place
That shows now not a single trace
Of sacrifices made for me,
That I might live a life that's free.

## Words of Love

*Love is a soft, compelling word*
*That wraps two hearts with a silken cord.*
*It gives with never a thought of gain,*
*Yet shackles your soul like a golden chain.*

*Love is a word that sets you free,*
*While still bringing you close to me.*
*It is the tie that ever binds,*
*Entwining hearts, possessing minds.*

*Love is a word that's generous, kind.*
*A gift, the like you will never find*
*Anywhere else in time or space,*
*It shines like a beacon on true love's face.*

## Forgotten

*Do you recognize that face,*
*Someone long ago embraced?*
*Standing in that stilted pose,*
*In those long outdated clothes?*

*Once these pictures were a treasure,*
*Bringing family members pleasure.*
*Now each one, on every page*
*Fades from memory with age.*

*What was the year? What was her name?*
*Now, they've all become the same;*
*Forgotten names, forgotten places,*
*Forgotten loves, forgotten faces.*

# Best Friends

*When he was small, he looked to me*
*For love, warmth and security.*
*In his small world, I was his god.*
*It only took a smile or nod*
*To send him into ecstasy*
*Over one small word from me.*
*And as he grew, there came to be*
*A test of wills, so he could see*
*Which one of us would be the boss.*
*And when we played a game of toss,*
*He'd take the ball and run away,*
*Pretending that he wouldn't play.*
*Now that we've both older grown,*
*It's as if we've always known,*
*When it comes down to the end,*
*This old dog is my best friend.*

# The Gift

*God gave me an angel*
*To love and take care of.*
*A precious little bundle*
*Sent from heaven above.*

*He put it in my keeping,*
*To cherish and to hold,*
*A gift worth more than rubies,*
*A value above gold.*

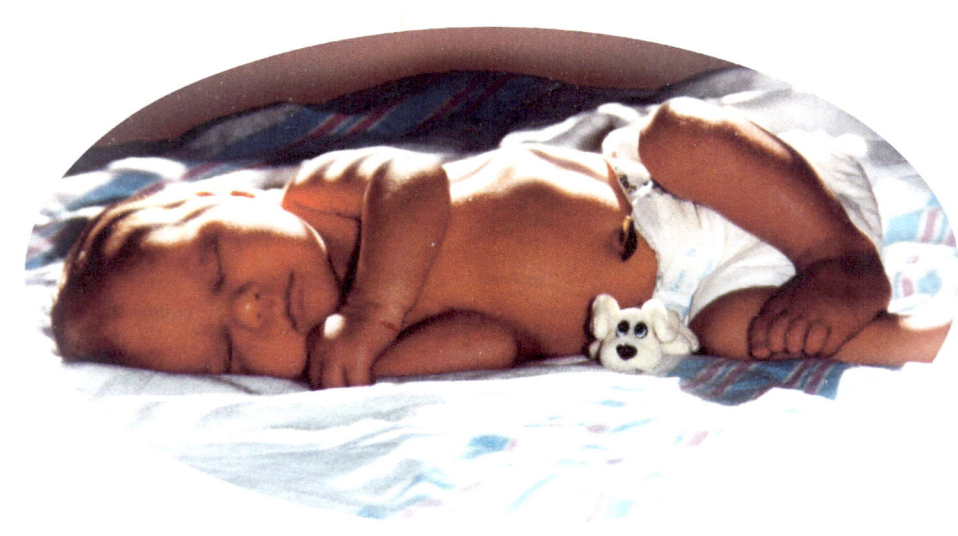

*I will nurture and protect it*
*Through happiness and strife.*
*I'll have it only briefly,*
*But love it all my life.*

*God gave to me an angel*
*To bring me special joy,*
*He blessed me with a child.*
*My darling, baby boy.*

# Little Golden Head

*I watch you sleeping, little son,*
*Your busy day, at last is done.*

*I gently stroke your rosy cheek,*
*My heart so full, I cannot speak.*

*I pray, while kneeling by your bed,*
*"God bless this little golden head."*

# Cuddle Me?

*"Cuddle me?", my darling said,*
*A questioning tilt to her tiny head.*
*So, I kissed her gently and held her tight*
*Before we finally said, "Good night".*

*"Cuddle me?" pleaded another child,*
*And the lonely heart within me smiled.*
*This echoing plea down the years*
*Is music to a mother's ears.*

*"Cuddle me?" haunts my memory*
*With thoughts of kisses given me*
*By children growing up with love*
*From Mother, Father, God above.*

*"Cuddle me?" should always be*
*A wish that's granted instantly*
*To children over all the earth,*
*From the moment of their birth.*

## Father's Lament

*I wish that we were closer, son.*
*When you were small and life was fun,*
*I know that you looked up to me,*
*To see the man you'd like to be.*

*But as you aged, we grew apart,*
*And though I held you in my heart,*
*There no longer seemed to be*
*That easy camaraderie.*

*Through the years, we both have grown.*
*You have a son now of your own.*
*Perhaps, our friendship we'll renew,*
*Now that you're a father too.*

## A Grandma's Prayer

*Bless, O Lord, this little one,*
*Whose life on earth has just begun.*
*Keep from fear, protect from harm,*
*Within the circle of Your arm.*

*Make life's pathway bright and clear,*
*For this precious child so dear.*
*Grant wisdom, Lord, love and health,*
*For these have value beyond wealth.*

*Endow your blessed, loving care,*
*And never let this child despair.*
*Pleasant dreams give without number,*
*Bestowed midst nighttime's gentle slumber.*

*Hear this Grandma's fervent prayer*
*And grant this babe the gift so rare*
*Of Thy eternal, boundless love,*
*Showered down from Heaven above.*

# Feline Friendship

*Furry friends through my life have tread,*
*Commandeering my food, usurping my bed.*
*Getting me up in the dead of night*
*To stumble around bereft of a light,*
*To open the door to the cold night air,*
*And watch and wait as they just stand there.*

*Why do I let them put me out so?*
*If you've ever had a cat, you'd know*
*How they twist and twine around your heart,*
*Causing you pain when it's time to part.*
*But, I'm willing to put up with shedding fur,*
*To hear the joy of a welcoming purr.*

# Angel In Disguise

*Little boy with golden hair,*
*Cheeks like roses, skin so fair,*
*Your eyes of brown melt my heart,*
*Piercing it with cupid's dart.*

*Those smiling lips curved like a bow,*
*Light your face with heaven's glow.*
*That happy laugh can hypnotize.*
*You're an angel in disguise.*

## Pictures

*Books of faded photographs*
*Sit dusty on the shelf.*
*I take them down and turn the page*
*To pictures of myself.*

*A time when I was small,*
*As you are now, my child.*
*A time when life was gayer,*
*Young and carefree, wild.*

*You wonder if I miss those times,*
*And hastily, I vow,*
*I was very happy then,*
*But I am happier now.*

## Angel Face

*The perfect curve of a silky cheek*
*Eyes of purest blue that peek*
*'Neath lashes with a gentle curl.*
*Who is this precious little girl?*

*Her soft lips form a cupid's bow.*
*She seems to shine with inner glow.*
*No one can ever take her place,*
*She is my darling, 'Angel Face'.*

## Wedded Bliss

*Through these years of wedded bliss,*
*Did you think it'd be like this?*
*The joys and sorrows, highs and lows*
*That we've shared. Remember those?*

*There were times filled with strife,*
*But love has always ruled our life.*
*Swiftly by the years have flown,*
*And always, dear, our love has grown.*

*So, on our anniversary day,*
*I fondly look at you and say,*
*"Darling, would you join me in*
*Doing it all once again?"*

## Missing You

*I miss you, dearest, when you're gone.*
*I need your presence dusk to dawn.*
*You are the other part of me,*
*The part that I'm most proud to be.*

*You are my lover and my friend.*
*Our bond endures, it knows no end.*
*To hear your voice gives me a lift.*
*When you are gone, I'm cast adrift.*

*Stay by my side, dear, never leave.*
*My heart, for you, would ever grieve,*
*If you should go and n'er return,*
*Eternally, for you I'd yearn.*

## Partners

*Our marriage is a partnership,*
*Once started there's no end.*
*From now until the end of time,*
*You are my lifelong friend.*
*Amazing, as the years go by,*
*How much we think the same,*
*United to the world we stand,*
*Playing out life's game.*
*Through our times together,*
*Sometimes we weren't in sync,*
*But never, in those tough times*
*Were we ever on the brink*
*Of calling quits, or giving up*
*All we've come to know.*
*It was just another phase*
*In life's ongoing show.*
*And still we travel on, my sweet,*
*Standing side by side,*
*Taking steps together*
*With love our constant guide.*
*In life you are my partner*
*And always it should be*
*That we will be together, dear,*
*Throughout eternity.*

# Friendship

*Friendship is a precious gift
That anchors you when cast adrift
By troubles that you can't surmount.
Friendship makes you feel you count
As special in the scheme of life,
And not a pawn of daily strife.
Friendship is a two-way street,
A bond that's shared when two friends meet.
You cannot be a friend alone,
It takes another who has known
You at your very worst and best,
And over time withstood the test
Of loving you, even in spite,
Of whether you are wrong or right.*

# Second Chance

*When they were small and I was young,
I often had no time for fun.
There was cleaning to do and bills to pay.
I rushed upon my busy way.
And when I tucked them in to sleep,
I'd obligations still to keep.
I kissed them and I turned away
My promises broken another day.
We had good times.  I loved them dear,
But interruptions grew each year.
Then suddenly, they'd grown and gone.
I felt like life's discarded pawn.
But then, a miracle. It's true.
This time I recognized my cue,
And let each precious moment be
Embraced and savored happily.
My children's children now I see,
Gathered sweetly at my knee.
I send an upward, grateful glance,
That God gave me a second chance.*

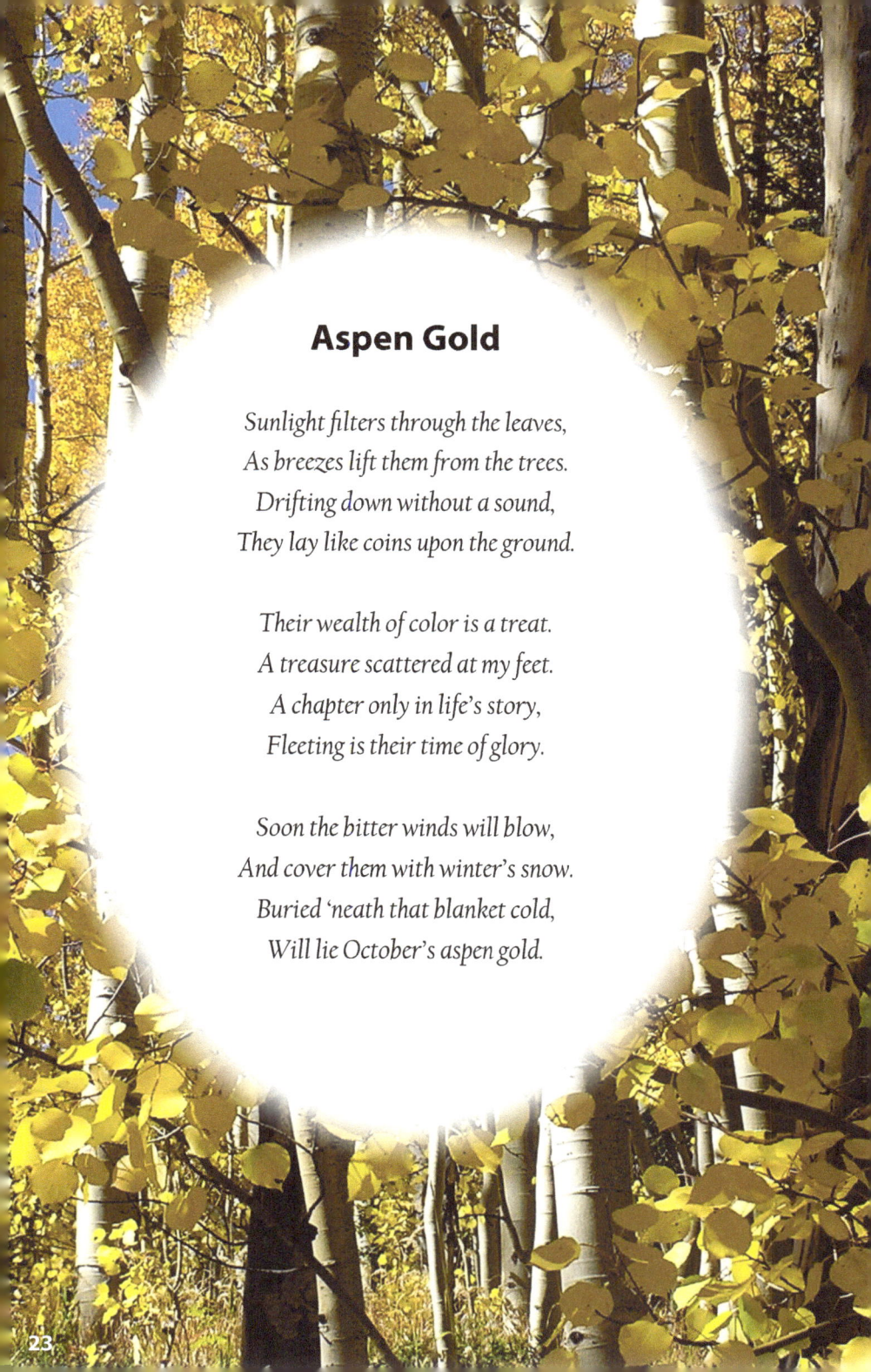

## Aspen Gold

Sunlight filters through the leaves,
As breezes lift them from the trees.
Drifting down without a sound,
They lay like coins upon the ground.

Their wealth of color is a treat.
A treasure scattered at my feet.
A chapter only in life's story,
Fleeting is their time of glory.

Soon the bitter winds will blow,
And cover them with winter's snow.
Buried 'neath that blanket cold,
Will lie October's aspen gold.

## Happy Face

*At the slightest attention from me,*
*His tiny face lights up with glee.*
*He waves his little hands about*
*And looks as if he'd like to shout*
*His happiness to one and all.*
*He's really having quite a ball.*
*Nothing can beat the joy he brings,*
*Not gold, nor other precious things.*
*His baby delight is quite contagious,*
*His expression of pleasure is outrageous.*
*He lights up every room in the place,*
*He's grandma's darling, 'Happy Face'.*

## Mother's Love

*My darling child, I feel your pain.*
*What will make you smile again?*
*I would take your greatest fear,*
*And make it mine alone to bear.*
*A mother's love will suffer long.*
*A mother's love is ever strong.*
*A mother's love will try to heal*
*Every hurt her child may feel.*

## Second Child

*You're not the first beneath my heart,*
*But still as much of me a part*
*As the one who came before,*
*A little girl whom I adore.*

*You're not the first child I have loved,*
*But I give thanks to God above,*
*For once again, He's blessed me so.*
*I just wanted you to know.*

*I long for you my unborn child,*
*By whom my heart is so beguiled.*
*I thrill to every move you make,*
*Yearning to hold you, my arms ache.*

*I await the dawning day,*
*When they come to me and say,*
*Here is your precious little one,*
*Your darling boy, your newborn son.*

## Always My Child

*I know, my dear,*
*You're fully grown,*
*And have a life*
*Of your very own.*

*But I will ever*
*Haunted be*
*By the child*
*You were at three.*

## Time for the Heart

The day was hectic and it seemed
Time I'd lost went unredeemed.
I struggled on with tasks galore
To finish each unending chore.

Patience gone, I sharply spoke
When he played a little joke
That he thought would make me smile,
And talk to him a little while.

He turned away, his shoulders shook
With silent sobs. I could not look
To see the blame within his eyes.
I felt my own tears start to rise.

I knelt beside him on the ground,
And turned my little man around,
As bowing down his small blond head,
"You hurt my heart", he softly said.

I swiftly pulled him to my breast,
His sobs now muffled on my chest.
My worldly cares were blown away.
It took a child to light my way.

## Guardian Angel

All around me I can feel,
A Heavenly presence that is real.
It guides my steps throughout the day,
Protecting me at work or play.
In everything I say and do,
I know my path is ever true,
For I will n'er in danger be,
While God's steward watches me.
And when I lay me down to sleep,
My safety lies within his keep.
From my side, please never stray,
Dear guardian angel, light my way.

## Soul Mates

My heart and mind
Are tuned to you.
Happy when you are,
Blue when you're blue.
Together, we form
Two halves of a whole.
Two bodies, two minds,
One heart, one soul.
And when my time
On earth is through,
I'll lie asleep,
Waiting for you.
Then, my dearest,
We will be
Soul mates
Throughout eternity.

## The Music of Memory

Another time, another place
Wraps my heart in fond embrace,
Times of sorrow, times of joy,
Passing years can n'er destroy.

I hug it all so close to me,
Enjoying things that used to be,
Savoring each time gone by
That made me laugh or made me cry.

When I am old and I am gray,
I'll treasure every passing day,
That comes flooding back to me
With each pleasant reverie.

Memories from down the years,
Bring to my eyes unshed tears.
Like music played upon a harp,
They pluck the strings within my heart.

# Heartbeats

*There are times in our lives that are as vital to us
as the beating of our hearts; times that thrill
and delight us, or bring pain and tears.
The nostalgia that wraps around your mind and soul
is like a soft blanket that warms and
comforts in times of happiness or stress.*

*The following verses run the full gamut of emotion;
joy and laughter, sadness and tears, nostalgia
and whimsy. These poems, like those
in Heartstrings, are meant
to touch those sentiments that are as much
a part of your life as your own heartbeat.*

*L. Diane Hindman*

## Heartbeats

*The nostalgia that you feel,*
*Whenever you recall,*
*Each cherished, fleeting moment*
*That held your life in thrall*
*With happiness or sadness,*
*Victory or defeat,*
*Makes them seem worthwhile,*
*Makes you feel complete.*
*Your memories are precious,*
*As much of you a part,*
*As each breath you take,*
*As the beating of your heart.*

## Treasures

*Each bit of paper, sandy shell,*
*And tattered picture too,*
*For my fading memory*
*Provides a unique clue*
*To times gone by, peaceful scenes,*
*And very special places,*
*Truly memorable events*
*And dearly beloved faces.*
*Each little scrap is a key*
*That lovingly unlocks*
*The depository in my heart*
*That is my treasure box.*

## My Closest Friend

*Honey, you're my closest friend.*
*I always know I can depend*
*On you. No matter what or where,*
*I know, sweetheart, you always care*
*About the ups and downs we've known,*
*And how much alike we've grown.*
*With each swiftly passing year,*
*I love you more each day, my dear.*

# Masquerade

*Do you really know who I am
Way down deep inside?
Can you even start to guess
The feelings that I hide?
I know you think I'm carefree,
And confident and bold,
You'd never guess the doubts
And fears that are untold.
I put on my public face
And meet the world head on,
While deep inside I wonder
If I am just a pawn
In the daily scheme of things
That life has in store,
And do I really matter,
And what am I here for?
Each of us has doubts
On what our life is worth,
And what God has planned for us
While we are on earth.
So, even though I seem to be
Poised and self-possessed,
I'm really biding time until
I pass His final test.*

# Christmas Joy

*Songs and laughter, filled with glee,
Toys beneath a glowing tree,
Stars that shine in children's eyes
Reflect the stars in winter skies.
Friends and family love abound.
Happiness is all around.
Christmas brings us joy and cheer,
That we will cherish through the year.*

# Hollyhock Dolls

*When I was small, my Grandma made*
*Hollyhock dolls as we sat in the shade.*
*We'd line them all up in a row*
*With inverted skirts arranged just so.*

*Flower buds formed their tiny heads*
*Above billowing skirts of brightest reds,*
*Or yellows, or white with pinkish hue,*
*A wonder to a child of two.*

*Their use was fleeting, but such fun,*
*'Til they withered away, one by one.*

# Rainy Day

*I hear the patter of the rain*
*Falling on my window pane,*
*Trickling down drop by drop,*
*It seems that it will never stop.*
*Melancholy, I turn away*
*To begin my busy day,*
*Tears, like raindrops stain my face*
*As I recall another place*
*And time, when our love was new,*
*And you declared you loved me too.*
*Time has passed since long ago*
*When you pledged you loved me so*
*That 'til eternity should come,*
*You and I would be as one.*
*How was it that we grew apart*
*Although I held you in my heart?*
*I stand alone and watch the rain,*
*Wishing you were here again.*

## Make Me Worthy

I wake up in the morning,
And bless the breaking dawn,
And thank You, Lord, for giving me
The strength to carry on.

Make me worthy, dearest Lord,
To be Your faithful child,
Ever constant in Your love,
Ever meek and mild.

Give me courage too, dear Lord,
To follow where You lead.
Help me, like Thee, to give my love
To those who are in need.

Let me meet this lovely day
With hope and strength renewed,
And be worthy, Lord, of You
In everything I do.

## Sky Hunter

*High above the world he wheels,*
*Slowly turning loops and reels,*
*Drifting on the currents of air,*
*Seemingly without a care.*

*Free of earthly bonds he flies,*
*Ever master of the skies.*
*Suddenly, he's downward bound*
*Like an arrow toward the ground.*

*Then to the sky, he climbs once more,*
*Returning there to glide and soar*
*Above the world in single flight,*
*Watchful in the morning light.*

## Love Ties

Love unites families and friends,
With a sacred bond that never ends.
It brings together hearts and minds
With the tie that ever binds
One soul to another for all time,
Mine to yours and yours to mine.
This special union will not bend,
It will be steadfast to the end,
A knot that cannot be untied
By anger, fear, or foolish pride.
And so, forever we will be
Bound by love, wholeheartedly,
Joined throughout eternity,
Me to you and you to me.

## Unsung Heroes

There are unsung heroes
That we see each day,
And we might not notice
Until they've gone away.
They do not call attention
To the things they do,
They just do it calmly
Without much ado.
They pack your lunch,
And wash your clothes,
And clean the whole house,
While blowing your nose.
They drive you to school,
And then grocery shop,
They're always so busy,
You'd think they would drop
From total exhaustion,
Caring so selflessly,
For those they love most,
Their own family.

## Think It Over

*When you're feeling overwhelmed*
*And nothing's going right,*
*If you're wondering what to do*
*But there's no help in sight,*
*Don't throw up your hands,*
*Or do something rash,*
*Remember that your fate can change*
*Within a lightning flash.*
*Don't feel sorry for yourself,*
*Stop and look around,*
*You're not really all alone,*
*There are others to be found*
*Who have walked along your path*
*And felt the way you do,*
*They have managed to survive,*
*And, darling, so will you.*

## Among the Angels

*In my dreams, I walk*
*Among the angels up above,*
*And feel the overwhelming*
*Strength of God's unending love.*
*And when I awaken*
*With the morning light,*
*I thank the Lord for being*
*With me through the night.*
*I know He'll stand beside me*
*In everything I do,*
*And when, at last, my time*
*Upon this earth is through,*
*I'll lay aside my burdens,*
*My trials and my care,*
*And sing the praises of Our Lord,*
*Among the angels there.*

# Unicorn

*Creature born of myth and light,*
*Imagination taking flight,*
*Denizen of a far off place,*
*In the mist of time and space.*

*Symbol of an age now gone,*
*Your fable lives in verse and song,*
*Our need for wonder satisfied*
*By beauty, grace personified.*

*In legendary, mystic dance,*
*Through the ancient ballads prance.*
*A fascinating lore you weave,*
*Enchanted legacy you leave.*

# Memory's Garden

*In my memory's garden grows*
*Flowers lovelier than any rose.*
*Laughing faces, kissed by sun,*
*Dew of tears when day is done.*
*They bloom eternal in my heart,*
*Forever, of my life a part.*
*Never fading, ever bright,*
*Always shining in the light,*
*Children's faces bringing pleasure*
*To this grandma's memory treasure.*

## The Visit

*He brought his little folding chair,*
*To sit and visit with her there.*
*He talked about the weather,*
*And the times they'd spent together.*

*He marveled at the flowers and trees,*
*And the coolness of the breeze.*
*He spoke of family and of friends,*
*And how it seems time never ends.*

*Then he rose as if to go,*
*And told her that he loved her so.*
*He turned away, his face was brave,*
*As he left her silent grave.*

## Forgiveness

*Forgiveness is a two way street,*
*Not cause for winning or defeat.*
*"I'm sorry", is just half the game.*
*"You're forgiven", cancels blame.*

*The sorrow for offenses done*
*Bodes no good for anyone,*
*Once forgiven it should be*
*Forgotten for eternity.*

# Armchair Traveler

*I travel to faraway places each day,*
*Meeting new people along the way.*

*I have adventures reserved for the brave,*
*Fulfilling the wander-lust that I crave.*

*With the heroine, I may know ecstasy,*
*With the hero, fight a battle at sea.*

*In my books, I live a vicarious life,*
*Of passion, adventure, triumph or strife.*

*And when I come home to my family again,*
*I tell them the wonderful places I've been.*

# Grandmother's Ring

*I put on my grandmother's ring today*
*And felt her presence from far away.*
*It gleamed as it did the day it was new*
*When she wore something borrowed and something blue.*

*It was as if I saw through her eyes*
*Each joy in life, each wondrous surprise,*
*The memories that once were hers*
*Flooded o're me from down the years.*

*I sensed the continuity*
*That linked the past and future to me*
*Held in the circle of her ring,*
*Like a symbol of life, a precious thing.*

# I Remember Mimi

*I remember well her smiling face,*
*Her throaty laugh, her stylish grace.*
*Twinkling eyes of deepest blue,*
*The stories that she told me too.*
*The scent of lilac in her hair*
*Though now turned gray, once was fair.*
*Her gentle touch that dried my tears,*
*Stays in my mind through the years.*
*Those loaves of bread on baking day,*
*The taste would take your breath away.*
*The flowers that she grew in spring*
*Flourished 'neath her nurturing*
*Like the children she adored,*
*Whom she considered God's reward*
*Showered down from Heaven above,*
*For a lifetime filled with love.*

## Poppa's Stories

When Poppa told me wondrous tales
About when he was young,
I could hardly wait each time
To hear my favorite one.
Stories of so long ago,
Of humorous things he did,
Chores he had and games he played
When he was just a kid.
He'd tell about the farm,
His friends and family,
The places that they went,
The things that they would see.
Everyone would gather 'round
When he began to tell
How he met his life long love,
And how hard he fell
For the sweet, young girl
Who would become his wife,
And how they worked together
To build a happy life.
I especially liked to hear
About when I was small,
Stories I was much too young
To be able to recall.
My Poppa has gone on now
To his last reward,
But I know he's telling stories
To his Heavenly Lord.

# By the Windmill

The morning sun stirs the breeze
That gently rambles through the trees,
And turns a bladed wheel around
With an ancient creaking sound.
Below the windmill, glowing green,
The loveliest garden you've ever seen
Wakes to greet the morning fair,
Its earthy fragrance fills the air.
Moving through this tranquil scene
A small blond head can be seen,
Bobbing up and down it goes
Like a bee from rose to rose.
Gathering bounty from the vines
That up a faded fence post winds
She clutches 'fussies' in her hand
To create a bouquet grand.
Now and then, she will stop,
And in her mouth a berry plop,
Wandering through summer's treasure,
Created just for her own pleasure.

# "Getting On"

*"How are you getting on?" they said.*
*I didn't tell them my soul was dead.*
*That I think of you every day and night,*
*They'd only tell me it wasn't right*
*To live in the past with a memory,*
*When there's so much in life to see.*
*If I told them, they'd only say*
*I really shouldn't live that way,*
*But "get on with life, put the past behind",*
*And wipe these tears from my heart and mind.*
*They'll never really understand*
*I still feel the comforting touch of your hand,*
*And see the smile on your loving face*
*And remember the warmth of your embrace.*
*I'll never go on without you, dear,*
*You'll be beside me each passing year,*
*Until the time when we will be,*
*United in eternity.*

## Too Many Words For Blue

*I don't know why I felt so sad,*
*Dejected, woeful, just plain bad.*
*I was depressed and melancholy,*
*Not a pleasant way to be.*
*Wretched, miserable, gloomy, glum,*
*As if tomorrow might never come.*
*Downhearted, unhappy, feeling low,*
*Just how dismal, you'll never know.*
*Disconsolate, despondent, sorrowful too,*
*I guess that I was downright blue.*
*I'm really feeling better now*
*Although I really don't know how.*
*You have been so very kind*
*To let me get that off my mind.*

# Rabbits' Dance

As I look out this winter's night,
There is a rare, enchanted sight.
Across the frozen ground I see
Shadows moving carefully.

Soft, they come upon the snow,
Hesitant, until they know
Danger's sleeping far away,
Until sunrise brings the day.

The moon looms large above the hill,
A silver glow casts shadows still
Upon the ghostly, white terrain
That stretches far across the plain.
They gather in a sheltered hollow.
One by one, the young ones follow.
Nose to nose, they seem to greet
Each other.  In a moment fleet
They whirl away as if in fright
And stare into the crystal night.
The air is crisp and crackles now,
Their figures seem to nod and bow.

Each rabbit is a small coquette,
In this bunny minuet.
Changing patterns do they weave,
Then one by one they slowly leave.

The moonlight on the snowy glade
Slowly now begins to fade,
As magic of the rabbits' dance
Is gone, within a single glance.

# Farewell

I'll miss you so, my dearest friend,
But friendships like ours never end.
So, with me you will always be
From now, through all eternity.

I'll hear your laughter on the breeze
As it rustles autumn's leaves,
And see the twinkle of your eyes
In the starry nighttime skies.

Your winsome smile will always be,
Shining in my memory
As I relive from day to day
The times we shared at work and play.

Though I no longer touch your hand,
I'll feel it's warmth and understand
That even if we're now apart,
You'll always live within my heart.

# Child of Stone

Just a figure carved in stone,
Not a child of flesh and bone.
Never to grow up, or old,
Never smiling, ever cold.
Features softened through the years,
By drops of rain and not by tears.
Marble skin warmed by the sun,
Not the childish face of one
Who runs, and laughs, and gaily plays,
And whiles away the summer days
Playing games in Heaven's field,
Leaving me with wounds unhealed.

## Silent Servants

*One small and dusty servant of God*
*Down the rocky roadway trod,*
*While on his back a woman-child*
*Lost in thought, gently smiled,*
*Aware of her awesome destiny*
*As she journeyed from Galilee*
*Toward the town of Bethlehem*
*Where she would bear the Savior of men.*

*Another time, many years gone,*
*In the midst of a wildly cheering throng,*
*Another silent servant of God*
*Down a different roadway trod,*
*Carrying now that woman's child,*
*A man of manner gentle and mild*
*Toward His awesome destiny,*
*To give His life upon the Tree.*

*Two humble servants with no voice,*
*These lowly creatures were the choice*
*Our Father used as instruments*
*In these related world events.*
*How then, might He use you and me*
*As testament for all to see*
*That God's love triumphs over all,*
*If we're obedient to His call.*

## Please Stay

*Love me again
Like you did before,
And I'll never ask
For anything more,
Except that you stay
One thousand years
To share my joys
And dry my tears.*

## Life Goes On

*I will be strong, I know I can
Meet the challenge now at hand.
I'll trust in God to see me through
In all the things that I must do.
Whether things go right or wrong,
I know that I must carry on.
So, bravely I'll hold up my head,
Dry my tears and smile instead.
I'll laugh to drive away the fear,
And when I look into my mirror
I'll know my efforts weren't in vain,
For I have learned to conquer pain,
And fear, and worry, sorrow too.
I know now there's life without you.*

# Transition

*Poised between tomboy and lady,*
*She's lively, boisterous and free,*
*Next minute she's shy and gentle,*
*And proper as proper can be.*

*The child that she is struggles*
*With the woman that she will become,*
*To hold on to these precious moments*
*Of childhood, so carefree and fun.*

*I cannot postpone the day*
*When she will no longer be,*
*That sweet and innocent angel*
*Who always had need of me.*

*So I will embrace the wonder*
*As into a woman she grows,*
*And welcome with arms wide open,*
*This beautiful, blossoming rose.*

## **Nests**

*Small homes of mud, twigs and leaves,*
*Built in the oak or under the eaves.*
*Shelters to cradle new families*
*Of eggs in groups of twos or threes.*
*Soon, there will be twittering pleas*
*From small naked babies ready to seize*
*Each morsel their parents bring to appease*
*Their fledglings, in nests, high in the trees.*

# I Can Fly

*In dreams, I soar into the sky,*
*And with a thrill, find I can fly.*

*Unfettered by earth's bonds below,*
*I'm free to follow where winds blow.*

*I feel the lift 'neath phantom wings,*
*And know now why the robin sings.*

*Such freedom is a heady fare,*
*This being lighter than the air.*

*For the moment I shed daily strife,*
*But dreams have a temporary life.*

# Cherubs

*Do cherubs into big angels grow?*
*That's something I would like to know.*
*Do Mommy angels sing them to sleep,*
*And pray to God their souls to keep?*

*Do they stay eternally chubby and small,*
*Or become magnificent and tall?*
*Do they frolic forever around God's throne,*
*Or do angels' work once they're grown?*

*I'd like to think that cherubs stay*
*Ever childlike as they play*
*At Heaven's gates, where they will greet*
*Each new soul, with laughter sweet.*

# Music

*Did you ever hum a lullaby*
*That brought a tear to your eye,*
*Or hear a pretty, lilting tune*
*That took you soaring to the moon?*
*Perhaps the soothing melody*
*Of a lovely symphony,*
*Or a schmaltzy love song*
*That made you want to sing along?*
*The gracefulness of the ballet*
*Moves me more than I can say,*
*While opera is such delight*
*I could attend most every night.*
*Waltzing puts me in a trance,*
*I can't wait to get up and dance,*
*Whirling on a ballroom floor*
*I would beg for more and more.*
*From hymns to jazz, square dance to swing,*
*Music makes our lives worth living.*

# Tribute

*Ever there, you always seemed*
*To sense my every need,*
*To pick me up when I failed*
*Your warning voice to heed.*

*You loved me when I didn't do*
*The things I knew I should,*
*And made me want, with all my heart,*
*To prove that I was good.*

*You lived your life in confidence,*
*Honest, loving, fair,*
*Teaching me what I should know,*
*Showing that you care.*

*You were there, close at hand*
*To prop up all my dreams,*
*Whenever things started to*
*Unravel at the seams.*

*You never seemed to require*
*The credit or the praise,*
*Things that really should have been*
*Yours in many ways.*

*I dedicate this tribute*
*To your faith in me, your calm,*
*And from the bottom of my heart*
*Say thanks, for being Mom.*

# The Storm

Dark clouds gather overhead,
Filling me with fear and dread.
I long to run to you and hide,
And feel your warmth close by my side.
I hear the thunder in my ears,
And try to hide my welling tears,
As lightning flashes all around,
I cannot make a single sound.
Please hear the words I long to say,
I hate it when we fight this way.

## It's Over

*How can it be over?*
*I tried hard not to fail.*
*We started out so happy,*
*Just like a fairy tale.*

*But then, the little doubts set in,*
*The tension and the strife,*
*I tried so hard to please you, dear,*
*To be the perfect wife.*

*You shunned all my efforts,*
*My pleas to reconcile,*
*To turn back time and capture*
*Our old love, for awhile.*

*Now, I sit and wonder,*
*What am I going to do?*
*I thought we'd be together,*
*Forever, didn't you?*

## Eternal Vow

*To you, I pledge eternal love,*
*No matter what befall,*
*My heart beats in time with yours,*
*At your beck and call.*
*United, we will face the world,*
*Each and every day,*
*As through the years we travel*
*Along life's busy way.*
*Our souls will always sing*
*In perfect harmony,*
*The melody of endless love*
*Fate wrote for you and me.*

# The Wall

*The wall is black as darkest night,*
*Yet, it reflects a moving sight,*
*A kneeling man, tears on his face,*
*A gentle healing taking place.*

*People drifting slowly by*
*Now and then, stop to cry*
*And touch a name upon the wall,*
*As their tears begin to fall.*

*Flowers pile up inches deep,*
*A tribute to eternal sleep*
*Of the ones whose lives were lost,*
*Who paid for peace, the highest cost.*

*Many, overcome with grief,*
*Visit here to find relief.*
*A puzzled child reaches out,*
*Wondering what it's all about.*

*God grant he'll never have to know*
*The reason why I'm weeping so.*

*(Vietnam War Memorial)*

## Comfort Me

*I reach for you in times of need,*
*Please be there for me when I plead*
*For your love and comfort, dear,*
*To chase away each childish fear.*

*When worries echo in my head,*
*Taunting me with unknown dread,*
*I need, my doubts, with you to share,*
*And know how much you really care.*

*Please comfort me, relieve this stress,*
*And restore my happiness*
*Which rests within your touch and smile,*
*And makes my every breath worthwhile.*

## With Each Beat

*I feel the beating of my heart*
*As memories begin to start,*
*And with each gentle, pulsing beat*
*Comes a recollection sweet*
*Of days spent laughing in the sun,*
*And nights of happiness and fun,*
*The crazy things we used to do*
*When we were young and love was new.*
*Each beat brings back with clarity*
*The hours we spent in ecstasy,*
*Dreaming of the days to come*
*When you and I would be as one.*
*Now that future is our past,*
*I can't believe it went so fast,*
*You are as much of me, a part,*
*As the beating of my heart.*

# Heartfelt

*Emotions of the heart; joy, sadness, patriotism, anger, happiness, sorrow, or bittersweet memories are but a few of the sentiments expressed in this poetry. Everything is not always 'hearts and roses', and some of our thoughts may be on the darker side from time to time. But, even though things may occasionally seem bleak, there is always a rainbow to look forward to after the storm.*

*These poems encompass the full spectrum of human feelings and I hope that one or two of them will touch a chord in your heart. May they mean as much to you as they do to me.*

*L. Diane Hindman*

*Heartfelt: Deeply felt; earnest, sincere.
(Webster's Dictionary)*

# Heartfelt

*I feel a love so deep and true*
*Every time I think of you.*
*You fill me with an endless bliss,*
*With your touch, your gentle kiss.*
*Emotions rise within my heart,*
*You have become of me a part*
*So necessary to my soul,*
*That without you, I am not whole.*
*Your smile, your laugh, your lilting voice,*
*Leaves my heart no other choice*
*Than to live the life I'm dealt,*
*A life of endless love, heartfelt.*

# Sacrifice

*He stares into the distance*
*As if he can hear,*
*The far off sound of guns*
*Echoing in his ear.*
*Would that he could forget*
*The agony and the fear,*
*That haunts him day and night,*
*Each and every year.*
*Never had he spoken*
*Of horrors he had seen*
*In those days, when he was young,*
*A boy of just eighteen.*
*Now he breaks his silence,*
*So you and I would know,*
*The sacrifices that were made*
*For us, so long ago.*
*He went to war expecting*
*To be brave and strong and bold,*
*What he found was pain,*
*And death, and terror cold.*
*Though he lost his youth*
*In far flung foreign lands,*
*He's proud his country's freedom*
*Rested safely in his hands.*

# Grandchildren

*Like lovely flowers 'round my feet,*
*They raise to me their faces sweet,*
*Each one as different as can be,*
*Each one a gift God granted me.*
*Filled with promise yet to come,*
*Securing their place in the sun,*
*I watch them as they run and play*
*Before their childhood fades away.*
*Mischievous boys with happy grins,*
*Cuts and scrapes on knees and shins,*
*Little girls' angelic smiles,*
*To comfort me across the miles,*
*And even when we're far apart,*
*I'll hold them always in my heart.*

# When I Loved You

*Your smile would melt my willing heart.*
*We could not bear to be apart.*
*I knew our love was ever true,*
*Long ago, when I loved you.*

*We shared the laughter and the tears.*
*We told each other all our fears.*
*You held my hand when I was blue,*
*Way back then, when I loved you.*

*Then the sunshine turned to rain,*
*I learned how not to feel the pain.*
*Gone was the glow that we once knew,*
*But I still thought that I loved you.*

*The sun still rises every day,*
*And I have learned to make my way.*
*I wonder if you're sorry too,*
*Remembering, when I loved you.*

# The Hug

He threw his arms around me
And took me by surprise,
I smiled to see the look
Of mischief in his eyes.
His impish grin caused me to ask,
"What was that hug for?"
"For no reason, Mom", he said,
And he was out the door.
I will always cherish
His spontaneous acts of love,
And save them in my memory
Within my treasure trove,
To call to mind each time
My world has come undone,
When I feel I need a hug,
Simply for no reason.

# A Perfect Stranger

I watched his face through hooded eyes.
Would he see through my disguise
I'm not what I pretend to be,
Not what he expects of me?
The person that I am inside,
Wants to run away and hide,
When he asks, "Do you love me?"
He sees just what he wants to see.
We live together side by side,
Bolstered by our foolish pride
That we know each other well,
And neither one of us can tell
What secret thoughts live in our mind,
Thoughts to which we both are blind.
Such is the mind-numbing danger,
Of living with a perfect stranger.

## The Sounds of Freedom

*What would freedom sound like*
*If freedom were a sound?*
*Would it be a beating drum,*
*Or something more profound?*
*Perhaps the flutter of our flag*
*As it waves in the breeze,*
*Or our national anthem,*
*Echoing through the trees.*
*The ring of children's laughter*
*Drowning out the blare*
*Of sirens racing through the streets*
*Warning us, beware,*
*Or the voice of disagreement,*
*Allowed to state its case,*
*Without fear of reprisal,*
*Without concern for race.*
*Its sound might be the absence*
*Of the guns of war,*
*The beauty of a silence*
*When men would die no more.*
*Whatever freedom's sound,*
*It sets us free from fear,*
*With a hand upon our hearts,*
*And music in our ear.*

# I Wish For You

I wish for you the bluest skies,
The light of love in someone's eyes,
The warmth of sun upon your face,
The safety of a strong embrace.

I wish for you freedom of choice,
A dream to make your heart rejoice,
The perfect trust of a child
On whom the grace of God has smiled.

I wish for you joy and laughter,
The happiness of ever-after,
Courage to face fear with pride,
And peace that comes from deep inside.

I wish for you a million things,
A life that gives your soul its wings,
Contentment in a job well done,
Respect and love from everyone.

Of all the wishes that could be,
There's one I'd like to guarantee;
A love to make your dreams come true,
This is what I wish for you.

## By Myself

I smile a lot and laugh out loud,
Gay and happy in a crowd,
Any stranger passing by
Would never, ever guess I cry
When I'm alone and by myself.

I put on a convincing act
And none would even guess the fact
That I hold down deep inside
A secret that I cannot hide,
When I'm alone and by myself.

There is no sorrow on my face,
Of my sadness there's no trace,
I hug my private pain to me
And I'm the only one to see,
When I'm alone and by myself.

Someday, my joy will be real,
And the happiness I'll feel
Will make my efforts all worthwhile.
I will not have to wear a smile
'Til I'm alone and by myself.

## White Lilacs

The heady scent of her perfume
Filled every corner of the room.
That fragrance still brings back to me
Far off days that used to be
When grandma smelled of lovely flowers,
As if enclosed by unseen bowers.
Her hands and face were soft as silk,
Her aging skin was white as milk,
And as I sat in her embrace,
I looked into her lovely face,
As sweet and beautiful to me
As blossoms on a lilac tree.
Each spring, when lilacs bloom again,
I think back, remembering when
I sat upon my grandma's knee,
And lilacs fill my memory.

# When Love Died

*You promised, dear, that you'd be mine,*
*From now, until the end of time.*
*You said you loved me, but you lied,*
*And something deep inside me died.*

*Your cruel words pierced my heart,*
*Tearing my whole world apart.*
*My tears flowed freely as I cried,*
*And a little more of our love died.*

*I feel the pain for all we've lost,*
*I don't know how to bear the cost,*
*That even though I know I tried,*
*You didn't care when our love died.*

# Touch My Heart

*Speak to me and touch my heart,*
*Miss me when we are apart.*
*Let me know how much you care,*
*Make me feel our love is rare.*

*Sing to me and touch my heart,*
*Let the gentle music start,*
*As you hold my hand in yours,*
*And we walk on golden shores.*

*Smile at me and touch my heart,*
*Let me be the work of art,*
*That you feast your eyes upon,*
*Until the light of life is gone.*

*Dream of me and touch my heart,*
*Call me darling, dear, sweetheart,*
*Stay beside me all the way,*
*And love me always as today.*

# Ode to Katie's Eyes

*Purest blue, like azure pools,*
*Shining like two precious jewels,*
*Lovelier than the summer skies*
*Is looking into Katie's eyes.*

*They sparkle with unfettered joy,*
*Her lashes flutter when she's coy,*
*Such innocence as lingers there*
*Makes this tattered world seem fair.*

*If I could look through Katie's eyes*
*I'd see a world of great surprise,*
*A world of wonder made for me,*
*Beckoning to a child of three.*

*All life's beauty at her feet,*
*All that is both good and sweet.*
*I see the splendor of the skies,*
*Reflected there in Katie's eyes.*

# Loneliness

*As time passes, so they say,
Missing him will fade away,
But right now, it's hard to see
Just how that can ever be.*

*I hear a laugh, full of glee,
And quickly turn around to see
A person that I do not know,
And it makes me miss him so.*

*I recall his smile, his walk,
How I loved to hear him talk,
It seems that he cannot be gone,
And I'm alone to carry on.*

*I cherish every memory,
Hugging them all close to me,
Holding emptiness at bay
Through each long and lonely day.*

# Then and Now

*I held you close against my heart
When you were but a child.
I sang your favorite melody,
And kissed you when you smiled.
Swiftly passed the days and years,
The child became a man.
You left to make your own way
According to God's plan.
It seems we've become strangers,
And sometimes I wonder how,
It ever came to be the way
That it was then, and now.*

## It Doesn't Hurt Anymore

It doesn't hurt me anymore,
When you walk out and slam the door.
I no longer sit and cry,
When I catch you in a lie,
And when you choose to be nice,
You leave my heart as cold as ice.
You treated our love carelessly,
To be discarded thoughtlessly,
And the love I felt for you,
Died each time you made me blue.
But, I no longer feel the pain,
So you have nothing left to gain
When you try to put me down,
And think that you can play around,
Because, I'm stronger than before,
And you don't hurt me anymore.

## Remember I Love You

When you're tempted to forget
How much I care for you,
Just look within your heart,
And you will find what's true.
No matter where you are,
Whatever may befall,
Remember, dearest one,
I love you, most of all.

## Apology

*I hear your voice, I feel your pain,*
*There's nothing I can do.*
*If I have caused the way you feel,*
*Then I am hurting too.*
*I can't seem to convince you,*
*That I meant no harm.*
*I did the best that I knew how,*
*I hold no magic charm*
*To change the future or the past,*
*There only is today,*
*And I can only hope that you*
*Believe me when I say,*
*That I will always love you,*
*No matter what befall,*
*And hope that you can see someday,*
*I'm human after all.*

## Tears in my Heart

*My eyes are dry,*
*I will not cry.*
*The hurt I'll hide*
*Down deep inside.*
*You'll never see*
*The pain in me,*
*And even though*
*You'll never know,*
*You were the start*
*Of the tears in my heart.*

## Going Home at Last

*We're going home at last,*
*The battles all are done.*
*We're not sure when the victory came,*
*But they say we won.*

*Through sacrifice and pain,*
*Through hardship and through tears,*
*We did the job we had to do,*
*And lived with all our fears.*

*All hail the mighty conquerors,*
*Heroes every one,*
*We've vanquished all our foes,*
*The fighting now is done.*

*We face a different battle,*
*With uncertainty ahead,*
*One we aren't sure we'll win,*
*An outcome that we dread.*

*Our lives have changed forever,*
*We must put this in the past,*
*And face the coming challenge,*
*When we go home, at last.*

# Heroes

*We admire the people who*
*Show courage in duress,*
*We think the deeds they've done,*
*Make them a great success.*

*But every day, there are those*
*Who do what they must do,*
*While no one sings their praises,*
*They are heroes too.*

*The men who go to their jobs*
*Every single day,*
*The wives and kids who wait for them,*
*And for their safety pray,*

*The man who will not stand aside*
*And watch injustice done,*
*The woman who without a word,*
*Sends to war, her son.*

*These are the world's true heroes,*
*Those who stand and wait,*
*And pray God will protect their own*
*From a fearful fate.*

*They do not ask for medals,*
*For fortune or for fame,*
*They merely do their duty,*
*And hero is their name.*

## Door to the Future

He stood before me at the door,
His eyes were riveted to the floor.
He did not move, he did not speak,
I suddenly felt my knees go weak.
Slowly, I reached out my hand,
And, although I had not planned
To touch him, I could not stop
As welling tears began to drop
Upon his slicked-down golden head.
The time that I had come to dread
Was here now, and I had to be
Brave for him, so he would see
The wondrous life he stood before,
Waiting just outside the door.

## The Eyes of Your Soul

Looking deep into your eyes
I see shining there,
The feelings that you have for me,
The deep love that we share.
Whenever we're apart, my love,
My heart begins to ache,
My very life begins with you,
You're every breath I take.
I need you always by my side,
Without you I'm not whole,
I live my life reflected in
The eyes that mirror your soul.

## The Rarest of Flowers

*God created an object of beauty*
*To bring delight to our eyes,*
*The velvet perfection of flowers*
*Adds pleasure to our daily lives.*
*The heart of a rose is pure,*
*Its beauty beyond compare,*
*Its delicate fragrance lingers,*
*Perfuming the nighttime air.*
*In the garden of lovely flowers,*
*Of radiant or gentle hue,*
*The one that surpasses them all,*
*The rarest of flowers, is you.*

# Shadows

*Softly on the powdered snow,*
*One by one, they silent go,*
*Pausing, watchful, now and then,*
*Ghostly, they glide on again.*
*The crescent moon casts a weak light,*
*That faintly radiates the night.*
*Revealing now in dim disguise*
*Shapes familiar to our eyes.*
*Vigilant always in the day*
*Though danger may be far away,*
*At night, they must more cautious be,*
*For there are perils they can't see.*
*Soundlessly, they pass from sight,*
*Gentle shadows of the night.*

## Our Love Will Last

*In this fast paced world,*
*Fads quickly come and go,*
*But one thing is enduring,*
*And here's what you should know.*

*I will always love you,*
*Whatever may befall,*
*No matter what we lose,*
*We still will have it all.*

*As long as we're together,*
*When time itself has passed,*
*We'll share this special gift,*
*A love, we know will last.*

## Bonds of Love

*The bonds of love cannot be severed*
*By the sword of death.*
*Dearest one, my love will last*
*Beyond my final breath.*

*And even though we each must make*
*That journey all alone,*
*You know I will be waiting there,*
*Welcoming you home.*

# You are My Brother

*The color of your skin
Is different from mine.
We are separated by
Ideas and space and time.
But underneath our skin
We are much the same,
We've many similarities
As we play out life's game.
We love our children and our homes,
Our flag and country too,
Whatever they might ask of us,
That is what we'll do.
We'd leave our families and our homes
To serve on foreign land,
And fight for what we believe
Is right and just and grand.
You may call me enemy,
And never call me friend,
But within our hearts
We are brothers in the end.*

# Old Friends

*They walk by at sunrise,
In evening, once again.
Inseparable companions,
I wonder where they've been.
It warms my heart to see
Their wordless comradeship,
As they get in shape
For an even longer trip.
The years have not been kind
To either of the pair,
But they still walk together
In stormy days or fair.
Their steps are slow and halting
As every day they go
To a destination,
Only they can know.
Their devotion to each other
Will last until the end,
When one will mourn the other,
Old man, old dog, old friend.*

# Did I Fail?

*Did I ignore your silent pleas,*
*Even though unspoken?*
*Did I say I'm sorry,*
*For promises I'd broken?*
*Did I recognize,*
*When you were in pain,*
*And do the very best I could*
*To make you smile again?*
*Did I praise you every day,*
*The way I knew I should,*
*And tell you how I thought,*
*That you are kind and good?*
*Did I fail to tell you,*
*That my heart stands still*
*At the mention of your name,*
*And it always will?*
*When a love is ignored,*
*Its passion quickly ends,*
*Is it now too late,*
*For me to make amends?*
*I see the things I should have done,*
*In vivid, clear detail,*
*And know I need not ask you,*
*Darling, did I fail?*

# I Chose You

*I chose you to share my life,*
*To be my love, to be my wife.*
*I chose you and you alone,*
*To live with me and be my own.*
*Though others may have gone before,*
*I'm now yours forevermore.*
*Never doubt and never fear,*
*I'll always be beside you, dear.*
*From now until eternity,*
*It will be just you and me.*
*Whatever I may say or do,*
*Remember, darling, I chose you.*

# Broken Pieces

*I watched a life break apart,*
*And it nearly broke my heart*
*To think that someone hadn't cared*
*To save the love that they had shared.*
*I watched those lives torn in two,*
*And wondered just what they would do*
*With the broken pieces now,*
*All that was left of their vow,*
*When they no longer could pretend*
*They'd love each other 'til the end.*
*I saw young lives that were shattered,*
*When love and faith no longer mattered,*
*And I cried that it was true,*
*Those lives belong to me and you.*

# Hearts of Steel

*They often carry their burdens alone,*
*And hold their heads up high.*
*They take the heartaches one by one,*
*And no one sees them cry.*
*They pour out love unselfishly*
*With no thought of return,*
*And never admit they need love too*
*Or how much they yearn.*
*They juggle jobs and chores and kids,*
*Devoid of any praise,*
*And do without the things they need*
*For years, and weeks and days.*
*They shoulder responsibilities*
*That would make others weak,*
*And when they're tired or feeling sad,*
*When everything looks bleak,*
*They stand up straight and bravely smile,*
*No matter how they feel.*
*They are the mothers of this world,*
*With hearts as tough as steel.*

## Walk in the Snow

*Pristine white, upon the ground it lies,
As wind through frosted branches softly sighs.
The air is filled with snowflakes falling down
To gently rest upon the frozen ground.
The world is cloaked in fluffy robes of white
That glitter in the fading winter light.
I wander in this chilly wonderland
And marvel how the world can look so grand.
The snow disguises ugly scars beneath
To display a haunting beauty, all too brief.
This blanket only covers for awhile,
Until erased by pale sun's melting smile.*

## Freedom's Flag

*Throughout this great, wide world of ours,*
*For me there's only one*
*Flag that stirs my heart,*
*From dawn to setting sun.*

*I see it wave against the sky,*
*It fills my heart with pride,*
*The values that it stands for*
*Will always be my guide.*

*Though all nations love their flag,*
*I'm sure you will agree,*
*This flag, with its stars and stripes,*
*Stands for all that's free.*

## Heart Songs

*Do you hear the melody*
*That plays within my heart?*
*Each time I see your loving face,*
*I feel the music start.*

*It swells to a crescendo*
*Whenever you are near,*
*When you gently touch my hand,*
*Or whisper in my ear.*

*At times I hear an angel choir,*
*A haunting, sweet refrain,*
*Like the sighing of the breeze,*
*Or patter of the rain.*

*Your presence near me always seems*
*To start a symphony,*
*Written for just you and me,*
*In two part harmony.*

## No Good-byes

*Say not farewell, only hello,*
*I'll be in your heart, wherever you go.*
*In fond memory, from near or afar,*
*My love will go with you,*
*Wherever you are.*

# Little Brother

At first you were a novelty,
That had nothing to do with me.
When I knew you were here to stay,
I wanted Mom to send you away.
But as time passed and you grew,
I started to get used to you,
And now and then it was fun
That I was not the only one.
As days went by and we grew older
I sort of liked having a brother,
Even though you could be a pest,
And put my patience to the test.
When I was sad or feeling blue,
I'd confide my woes to you.
You always made me feel you cared
About the worries that I'd shared.
Throughout the years, we've both grown,
And now have families of our own.
We'll always have a special bond,
Through this life and beyond.

# WTC Remembered

The setting sun shone blood-red
As nations mourned uncounted dead.
The events of that fateful day
Took the whole world's breath away.
With one heart we felt the pain
For those we'd never see again,
And as we grieved our souls craved
Revenge against those so depraved
That they would rain such horror on
The innocents who died that dawn.
May all countries now unite
In the sacred cause of right,
And wipe all hatred from our shores,
Throwing open freedom's doors.
Let pain and fear and terror cease,
That humankind may know true peace.

# Love Is A River

Love is a river that sometimes flows
Gently, as trickling on it goes,
Tumbling at a merry pace,
Never mindful of time or place.

Love is a river bubbling along,
It's melody a happy song,
Lifting us to a dizzying height,
Surrounding us with dazzling light.

Love is a river, wild and free,
A torrent, engulfing you and me
With passions we cannot suppress,
An endless stream of happiness.

Love is a river to fill the heart,
Knowing we will never part,
But sail on through eternity,
Until we reach love's final sea.

# Heart-2-Heart

*The poems in this section of poetry are a mixed
collection of thoughts, experiences and
emotions. Each one is an attempt to put
into words my feelings or that of those around
me at the time. They have no particular
theme except that they come from my
heart and I hope they touch something
deep within your own heart.*

L. Diane Hindman

"Heart to heart: forthright, frank."
Webster's Dictionary

## Heart to Heart

*Words can never tell you
Just how much I care.
You will feel it, deep inside,
If you really dare
To open up your heart,
And welcome my love in,
Only then, my dearest,
Can true love begin.
And in that magic moment,
You will feel the start
Of the glow that comes from
Living heart to heart.*

## Kaleidoscope

*Life's a kaleidoscopic whirl.
You only have to give it a twirl
And it can spin your life around,
Turning everything upside down.

The dizzy changes cloud your mind,
Hiding the path you are trying to find,
Obscuring your reason, causing doubt
That you really know what life's about.

Our Lord's path is straight and true,
And He will show you what to do.
Trust in Him and heed His Word,
And your salvation in assured.*

## A Sweetness of Heart

*His brash demeanor protects him*
*From callous humankind,*
*That dictates every man and boy*
*Leave gentleness behind.*

*They always show how tough they are,*
*No matter how unreal*
*That emotion is to them or*
*How they really feel.*

*They never hug and never cry,*
*And never show they care.*
*It really doesn't matter that*
*It is so unfair.*

*As a defense from ridicule,*
*They never will confess*
*They harbor deep within their hearts,*
*Love and tenderness.*

*You must look past the bluster*
*To find what's really true,*
*This hidden sweetness of the heart*
*Is shown to very few.*

# Across the Miles

*I will always think of you*
*As a special part of me,*
*Someone who encouraged me*
*To be what I could be.*
*You'll never be forgotten*
*When you're far away,*
*And though we won't talk often,*
*I'll think of you each day.*
*I'll miss the visits that we had,*
*The smiles and, yes, the tears,*
*The friendship that we forged*
*O're these many years.*
*Though the miles between us*
*May seem a distance far,*
*My heart will travel with you,*
*No matter where you are.*

# The One Who Loves You

*Who will always be there
When you need a friend?
Who's the one you'll count on,
Until the very end?
Who overlooks your faults
And loves you anyway?
Who will wipe away your tears,
And never, ever say,
That they told you so,
When you ignored again
The sage words of advice
You should have taken then?
Who loves you without a doubt,
Or speck of condemnation,
And would gladly die for you
Without hesitation?
You shouldn't have to guess
Who that one might be,
You only need to turn around,
To see that one is me.*

# Way Back When

*When I remember "way back when",
I wish I were a kid again.
Carefree days would come and go,
With summer sun or winter snow.
The seasons blended one by one,
Until my years of youth were done.
Now, I look back as through a mist,
Did they, in actual fact, exist?
Or is it just a wistful dream,
And things aren't really what they seem,
But painted with the brush of time
Appear to be the more sublime?
I hope the years will not erase,
Nor reminiscences replace,
But let me keep this memory
Of the way things used to be,
Alive and well within my mind,
And leave reality behind.*

# Cowboy Dreams

When I was young, I had a dream,
To be a tough cowboy.
I'd ride the range and rope those cows,
Just like the real McCoy.
My childish mind built visions
Of nights beneath the stars,
Of days of riding herd,
And fights in small town bars.
My daily speech was peppered
With salty quotes and slang,
Like, "thank ya mam" and "shore 'nuf",
"Lil' doggies", "nope" and "dang".
But time has ways of changing things
I'm sure you will agree,
The open range became a lawn,
My horse an SUV.
I still have the wanderlust
To live life wild and free,
But now I have to be content
To watch it on TV.

# Reunion

My heart beats fast, my hands are wet,
And I haven't talked to anyone yet.
My face is plastered with a grin,
I feel like I'm sixteen again.
Do you think anyone can tell
That I'm just as scared as hell?
Is that the guy I used to know,
Who said he'd always love me so?

That woman there was my best friend,
We pledged our friendship to the end,
But neither of us ever wrote,
And now we both feel quite remote
From the good times and the bad,
All the adventures that we had.

It really does seem sort of strange,
The way our lives get rearranged
From what we thought that we would be
In those days when we were free
Of doubts about what we could do,
And things that we believed were true.

It's nice to see them all again,
And remember way back when
We all were young, and full of hope.
Now we're just glad if we can cope
With challenges faced every day,
And all the bills we have to pay;
The car repairs, the kids, the rent,
The bank account we've overspent.

It all at once seems far away,
As we return to yesterday.

## Lest We Forget

*Raise our nation's flag on high
As tribute to all those who try
To understand the reason for
The ragged sound of cannon roar.
Lest we forget.*

*Hold your children to your heart,
For they may someday be a part
Of the pain accompanying wars,
When loved ones die on far off shores.
Lest we forget.*

*Remember, there's a price for peace.
May hate and fear and anger cease,
Replaced with freedom's gentle song
That sooths away the hurt of wrong.
Lest we forget.*

*Allow our tears to freely flow,
And may our bitter losses show,
The depth of sorrow that we feel
Before our souls can start to heal.
Lest we forget.*

# Preservation

*Behold the wonders of this earth,*
*Ere they turn to dust.*
*Are your eyes too blind to see*
*Beneath the filth and rust?*
*Each and every precious gift*
*Should carefully be reserved*
*For generations yet to come.*
*They must be preserved.*
*The beauty that is here for us,*
*We must strive to save.*
*This is the only home we'll have,*
*This side of the grave.*

## Meditation

*With eyes lightly closed, I sit in the sun,*
*Anticipating the moment to come*
*When all my tensions will melt away,*
*And I can face the rest of the day.*

*A quiet wind caresses my face*
*As I lose all track of time and place.*
*Peaceful thoughts soothe my mind,*
*Leaving the chaos of life behind.*

*My breathing is one with the gentle breeze*
*As my mind softly rustles the whispering leaves.*
*My spirit reflects the warmth from above,*
*A tangible gift of Heavenly Love.*

*My heart and soul are subtly renewed.*
*Earthly troubles no longer intrude*
*To bind me to the turmoil and strife*
*That threatens to overwhelm daily life.*

## Easter Prayer

*Blessed Savior, Lord of Light,*
*Who dispelled the death of night,*
*Take away our sinful ways*
*And grant salvation all our days.*

*Wash us clean as fallen snow,*
*Show us the truth we should know,*
*That Your gift be not in vain,*
*Until You come to earth again.*

# Your Best Friend

*Be good to yourself,
You're the best friend you've got.
Friendships like that
Can never be bought.
Always try
To be kind to yourself,
Don't place your dreams
High on a shelf.
Look for good things
To happen to you,
And you'll be prepared
Whenever they do.
How can you expect
To treat others with care,
If, to yourself,
You are never fair?
The person who values himself
Will agree,
When you love yourself,
You'll be all you can be.*

# What is in Your Heart?

*Tell me what is in your heart,
For I can't seem to see
The love I hope is hidden there,
Waiting just for me.*

*Looking deep into your eyes,
I'm longing to see there,
The glimmer of affection,
That shows you truly care.*

*Tell me, dearest, that you feel
The passion that I do,
A deep, abiding adoration,
Like I feel for you.*

*I couldn't bear the pain,
If you don't care for me
The way I'll care for you, dear,
Throughout eternity.*

## Help Me, Lord

*I'm doing the best I can, dear Lord,*
*To live the way I should.*
*I always try my very best*
*To be both kind and good.*
*I know my life is in Your hands*
*And I should place my trust*
*In You, to help me tread Your path,*
*And do the things I must.*

*I want to live as You did,*
*Even though it's hard*
*To avoid temptations*
*That constantly bombard.*
*There are many barriers*
*I find along my way,*
*And life throws up more obstacles*
*Each and every day.*

*Give me patience please, Oh Lord,*
*Help me not to try*
*To face each challenge on my own,*
*When I should rely*
*On Your strength to get me through*
*Each test that I must meet,*
*'Til I can lay my burden*
*At my Savior's feet.*

## Open My Eyes

*Open my eyes, Lord, that I may see,*
*The wonders you have in store for me,*
*The amazing world in which I live,*
*The bounty that it has to give.*

*Open my mind, Lord, that I may know*
*The secrets You desire to show*
*To those who heed Your gentle call,*
*Who give to You their best, their all.*

*Open my heart, Lord, that I may feel*
*The truth of what is good and real.*
*May I be the vessel that You choose*
*To carry forth Your joyous news.*

*Open my soul, Lord, and let love flow,*
*Let it blossom, let it grow.*
*May I reflect Your love and grace,*
*'Til I gaze, at last, upon Your face.*

## Redemption

*I thought I could handle it on my own,*
*But I failed.*
*And when I found I was all alone,*
*My heart quailed.*
*I thought I didn't need a helping hand,*
*But I did.*
*I felt no one could understand,*
*So I hid.*
*My life and confidence were shattered,*
*And I cried.*
*At last, I decided nothing mattered,*
*But I lied.*
*When I'd reached the end of my rope,*
*Then I prayed.*
*That's when my Lord gave me hope,*
*And I was saved.*

## My Prayer

*Give me, Lord, the patience I seek.*
*Please strengthen me, for I am weak.*

*Guide me in the way I should go,*
*Grant me wisdom that I may know*
*The things that You expect me to do,*
*And what things I should leave to You.*

*Console me, Lord, and dry my tears,*
*Help me to overcome my fears*
*Of a future that lies ahead*
*With unknown things that I dread.*

*Bless me, Lord, when I fail,*
*For this mortal flesh is frail,*
*And quakes at tasks that seem too great*
*When understanding comes too late.*

*Forgive the wrongs that I have done.*
*I know that You're the only one*
*Who can save me from mistakes*
*Which would only cause heartaches.*

*Heal me, Lord, when I'm in pain,*
*May my plea not be in vain,*
*But lift me up and let me be*
*Comforted, Oh Lord, by Thee.*

## A Light in the Dark

I stumbled and I fell,
Because I could not see
Through the dark and gloom,
What lay ahead for me.
I struggled on, hopelessly,
Searching for a way
To stay upon the path,
And not be led astray.
Helpless, fearful, groping,
I'd given up all hope
Of reaching a safe refuge,
I could no longer cope.
Then through the blackness, faintly,
A flickering ray of light
Revealing all before me,
Pushing back the night.
Suddenly, the way was clear,
The shadows all had flown,
My Lord reached out His hand to me
And gently led me home.

## Regret

Hands thrust in his pockets,
He stood there looking down
At withered flowers strewn upon
The bare and fresh turned ground.
His workman's hands were still,
Tears lay on the cheek
Of this strong and forceful man,
Whom sorrow had made weak.
His broad shoulders now were bent,
His balding head was bowed.
This man, once brash and certain,
Now stood and sobbed aloud.
He'd lost a gift more precious,
Than he could ever know,
And now he'd missed the chance,
To ever tell her so.

## If God Made Eve First

*If God made Eve first,*
*Would there be less strife,*
*Less fear, less pain,*
*A happier life?*

*If God made Eve first,*
*Would women still cry*
*When the man in their life*
*Bid them good-bye?*

*If God made Eve first,*
*Would there be more love?*
*Would sorrow and sadness*
*Become unheard of?*

*If God made Eve first,*
*Would I now be free*
*Of the painful hurt*
*That you have caused me?*

*If God made Eve first,*
*Would we ever want more?*
*So what in the world,*
*Would we need Adam for?*

# Betrayed

*In the night, I turn away*
*As you softly cry.*
*I cannot reach to comfort you,*
*I think that you know why.*
*My heart is numb with pain suppressed,*
*As I recognize*
*That we have reached the final stage*
*In our shattered lives.*
*When you revealed the lies you'd told,*
*My mind went into shock.*
*You treated our love casually*
*With your idle talk.*
*The value of the love we shared*
*You seemed to ridicule.*
*You threw away the joy we had,*
*You broke the golden rule.*
*The damage, dear, that you have done*
*Cannot be repaired.*
*Would this have ever happened*
*If you'd really cared?*

# Only a Dream

*Deep in the darkness of the night,*
*I beheld a gleam of light*
*That slowly grew to fill the room,*
*Dispelling every trace of gloom.*
*At its center, seemed to glow*
*A smiling face I used to know.*
*Memories came back to me,*
*Of loving arms that used to be*
*Wrapped around me in embrace,*
*A gentle kiss upon my face.*
*My mind was filled with quiet peace,*
*My lonely heart felt sweet release.*
*Then it faded from my view*
*And as I awoke, I knew*
*It wasn't real as it had seemed,*
*But only something I had dreamed.*

# Storms

When I was just a child,
I feared each gathering storm.
I'd run inside and hide my head
When clouds began to form.

But, when I grew older,
I conquered childish fright,
I knew the sound and fury
Would somehow be all right.

Other storms would rock my world,
And challenge me to stand
Strong against cold winds of fear,
My courage in my hand.

At my side, my Lord and Friend,
Helps me face each storm,
And in the bosom of His love,
My world stays safe and warm.

## I Pray for You

I pray for you to be content
With a peace that's heaven sent.
I pray that God, your life will bless,
And bring you joy and happiness.

I pray the Lord will give you peace
And grant that you find sweet release
From daily tension, anger, doubt,
'Cause that's not what life's all about.

I pray to God to calm your mind,
And leave all pain and fear behind.
I pray that He will ease your life,
And make it free of stress and strife.

I pray for you a healing balm,
A lasting ease, a soothing calm,
Restful, gentle thoughts that give
A life that is a joy to live.

And when He gives these things to you,
When all my fervent prayers come true,
I pray that you will, in return,
Teach to others what you've learned.

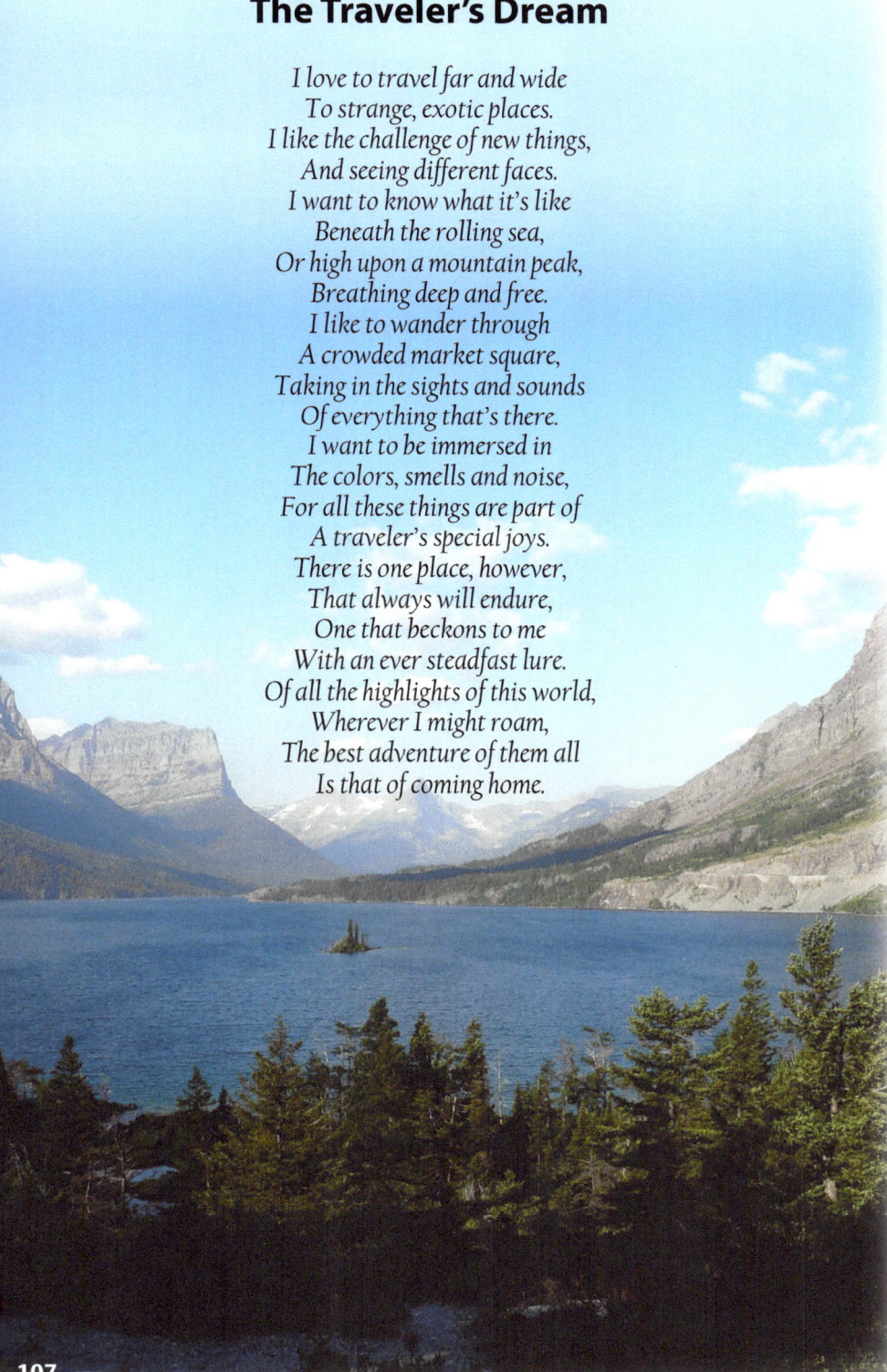

# The Traveler's Dream

I love to travel far and wide
To strange, exotic places.
I like the challenge of new things,
And seeing different faces.
I want to know what it's like
Beneath the rolling sea,
Or high upon a mountain peak,
Breathing deep and free.
I like to wander through
A crowded market square,
Taking in the sights and sounds
Of everything that's there.
I want to be immersed in
The colors, smells and noise,
For all these things are part of
A traveler's special joys.
There is one place, however,
That always will endure,
One that beckons to me
With an ever steadfast lure.
Of all the highlights of this world,
Wherever I might roam,
The best adventure of them all
Is that of coming home.

# First Teacher's Conference

As I wait with baited breath,
My palms are wet, I'm scared to death.
I'm not sure what she'll want from me.
What might she expect I'll be?

A virtuous paragon I'm not,
A tower of strength? What a thought!
I'm just an ordinary Mom
Trying hard to remain calm.

I hope that she will be impressed,
I wore my most becoming dress,
So that he'll be proud of me
When I meet the "powers that be."

I pray that I can pass the test,
I really want to do my best
When I meet this woman who
Thinks that he is special too.

At least, we both think alike,
He's such a darling little tyke.
I can't believe he's in first grade.
What amazing progress he has made.

Here she comes, I don't know how,
But I'm feeling relaxed now.
She smiling, and she seems to be
Actually pleased to see me.

Now that we're standing face to face,
I don't feel so out of place.
I think it's going to be okay,
I've lived through his first conference day.

# Carousel

*Wooden horses spinning round,*
*Gaily rising up and down.*
*Dancing to a jolly tune,*
*The ride is over much too soon.*

*Prancing horses making dreams,*
*As we wildly turn, it seems*
*Worldly cares are spun away,*
*To be forgotten for a day.*

*Painted horses through the years,*
*Witness children's laughter, cheers,*
*Delighting in the fun they've found*
*riding on a merry-go-round.*

## Three Wishes

If I could have three wishes
That would all come true,
I would wish, my child,
These three things for you.

First, I'd wish that peace be yours
To calm your restless soul,
A healing balm to touch your life,
And make your spirit whole.

Next, I'd wish you joy in life,
The kind that will endure,
Like the love of God,
Unceasing and secure.

My final wish is happiness
In everything you do,
To fill your world with laughter,
That lasts your whole life through.

If I could have three wishes,
And they all came true,
These are what I'd wish,
My dearest child, for you.

# School Dance

*She stood there waiting patiently,*
*A smile on her face and a scab on her knee.*
*Her hair had been brushed 'til it shone like gold,*
*You'd never guess she was 12 years old,*
*Except for her shy and nervous glance*
*Toward the boy in baggy pants.*

*They both pretended not to care*
*Whether or not the other was there.*
*Then, with a look that seemed like dread,*
*He shuffled forward and hung his head*
*As he mumbled to her with obvious fear,*
*The words that she had been waiting to hear.*

*"Ya wanna dance?"*

## Columbia

Higher than eagles soared their flight
Into a darkness black as night.
Striving upward, ever higher,
Expanding the bonds of mans' desire
To touch the universe beyond
This earthly coil to which we're bound.

Like legendary queens and kings,
Their courage rode on silver wings
To do battle in the vast unknown,
Ascending to their starry throne
To reign victorious at the helm
Of that airless, endless realm.

Their crusade ended, now they turned
Toward the home for which they yearned.
Conquering heroes, one and all,
Answering the siren call
Of that glowing globe of blue,
Calling to the tried and true.

Their homecoming was not to be.
In bursts of flame their souls broke free.
Like angels returning to the sky,
Their valiant spirits rose on high
To live eternal, for all time,
In every legend, song and rhyme.

## All Hallows' Eve

Stark against the moonlit sky
Stand the naked trees,
Reaching up with longing arms
For their fallen leaves.
The wind moves through the barren boughs
Moaning deep and low,
Dire predictions, cold and bitter,
Of the coming snow.

Small shadows flit from tree to tree
Rustling as they go,
Furtive in an endless quest
Only they can know.
From the darkness now they dash,
Converging on the prize,
And as they come into the light
You see their glittering eyes.
Strange, unusual creatures loom
Before my open door,
"Trick or treat, trick or treat",
In unison they roar.

# Island in the Sun

Mountains raise their sun-drenched heads
Above the glassy sea,
As gentle tropic breezes whisper
Ageless songs to me.
Songs that tell the ancient tales of
Men that came before,
To find forgotten treasures
Upon this timeless shore.
The ocean waves beckon me
With their sirens' call,
To abandon worldly cares
That hold my soul in thrall.
Overhead, snow white birds
Wheel effortless in flight,
As the sun sinks in the sea
Giving way to night.
The stars, like holes in velvet black,
Rise to rule the dark,
Paying tribute to the moon
With each tiny spark.
This is my island in the sun,
My perfect paradise.
To own my heart forevermore
Is its only price.

## Renewed Trust

Her touch is gentle, tender,
As she softly speaks
In a low, assuring voice,
Against his fuzzy cheek.
His tension seems to ease,
As he leans forth to hear,
The loving words she has to say
In his twitching ear.
His fur is silky to the touch,
But wasn't always so,
He's suffered cruel treatment
Only he can know.

But, now he tries to trust this child
Who touches him with love,
Accepting offered kindness,
He hasn't had much of.
Deep within his furry throat
Comes a contented sound,
A rumble deep and low
Of ecstasy profound.
He's found a haven safe,
From fear and loneliness,
One that he can count on,
A place of happiness.

## Come Back to Me

My heart goes dancing on the waves,
Across the deep blue sea.
I hear you call from foreign shores,
"Please come back to me".
A melody, haunting, sweet,
Lulls me into sleep,
In my dreams, I see your face,
And silently, I weep.
Through my feverish mind
repeats this single litany,
"I miss you so, my dearest one,
Please come back to me".
Restlessly I toss upon
My solitary bed,
Longing for your gentle touch,
Remembering what you said,
"No matter where you roam,
O're land or sky or sea,
I will always love you, dear.
Please come back to me."

## Let Go and Let God

*I suffered sorrow day by day.*
*It seemed that I was doomed to pay*
*For the wrongs that I had done,*
*It felt as if my sins had won*
*And damned me to eternal hell.*
*My grief and fear I could not quell.*
*At last, I knew, that on my own*
*I could not save myself alone,*
*In God I had to place my trust,*
*His judgment would be swift and just.*
*My life was mired in deep despair,*
*I knew there was no one to care*
*If I lived, or if I died,*
*And in my pain, to God I cried,*
*"Help me Lord. Please hear my plea,*
*And send Your Grace to comfort me."*
*I bowed my head and gave to Him*
*All the agony within.*
*I forfeited my heart and soul*
*To my Lord, to be made whole.*
*The heavy burdens that I bore*
*Now would trouble me no more,*
*I've left the path of sin I'd trod,*
*Now I've let go and let God.*

# The End

*Look for*
*Spiritual Reflections From My Heart*
*by L. Diane Hindman*

www.ingramcontent.com/pod-product-compliance
Lightning Source LLC
Chambersburg PA
CBHW042336150426
43195CB00001B/4